Drawing Your Stress Away

OTHER BOOKS & AUDIO PROGRAMS BY LUCIA CAPACCHIONE

Hello, This Is Your Body Talking: A Draw-It-Yourself Coloring Book (Swallow Press/Ohio University Press)

The Creative Journal: The Art of Finding Yourself, 35th Anniversary Edition (Swallow Press/Ohio University Press)

The Power of Your Other Hand (New Page/Career Press)

The Creative Journal for Teens (New Page/Career Press)

The Creative Journal for Children (Shambhala)

The Creative Journal for Parents (Shambhala)

Recovery of Your Inner Child (Simon & Schuster)

Visioning: Ten Steps to Designing the Life of Your Dreams (Tarcher/Putnam)

The Art of Emotional Healing (Shambhala)

The Inner Child Playbook (e-book, at LuciaC.com)

The Talent Workbook (e-book, at LuciaC.com)

The Wisdom of Your Other Hand (5 CDs, at LuciaC.com)

The Picture of Health (CD, at LuciaC.com)

The Sound of Feelings (CDs with Jessie Allen Cooper's music, at LuciaC.com)

Visioning® (Musical accompaniment for the Visioning® process, at LuciaC.com)

TO CONTACT LUCIA CAPACCHIONE:

Visit: www.LuciaC.com & www.visioningcoach.org

Call: (805) 546-1424

Email: LuciaCapa@aol.com

Write to Lucia Capacchione at P.O. Box 1355, Cambria, CA 93428

For information about Creative Journal Expressive Arts Certification training with Dr. Lucia Capacchione & Dr. Marsha Nelson: www.LuciaC.com—Professional Training

Drawing Your Stress Away

A DRAW-IT-YOURSELF COLORING BOOK

The Creative Journal Approach

Lucia Capacchione, PhD, ATR, REAT

Swallow Press 🗲 Ohio University Press

Athens

Swallow Press
An imprint of Ohio University Press, Athens, Ohio 45701
ohioswallow.com

Printed in the United States of America
Swallow Press / Ohio University Press books are printed on acid-free paper ∞ ™

27 26 25 24 23 22 21 20 19 18 17   5 4 3 2 1

"New Life Pushes Up" original drawing (page 48) and page of reflective journal writing
courtesy of Claire M. Perkins.

Time-life mandala drawing (page 90) courtesy of Jennifer Svendsen Delaney.

Contents

Introduction

Drawing Your Way to Health

This is a Draw-It-Yourself Coloring Book. There are no lines to color inside. No pictures to fill in. No ready-made patterns or designs to follow.

The only lines in this coloring book are the ones you make.

If you are like most people, you are probably thinking, *Oh no, I can't draw. I don't have any talent. I'm just not creative.* Isn't that what traditional coloring books are for? You just color away and don't worry about the artistic merit of the lines. After all, the lines were done by somebody else. A real artist!

That was old-school. This is **the *new* coloring book.** Here you'll make art that comes from the inside out, not from the outside in. These scribbles, doodles, designs, and drawings come from you. They express your feelings, unique experiences, dreams, and wishes. **In *the new coloring book* you get to ex-press, de-stress, and relax in a safe place free from judgment and criticism.**

Let's face it, fear of drawing comes from a Critical voice in your head that says:

You can't draw (like Rembrandt or Van Gogh or whoever).

You don't have any talent. You'll make ugly art. You'll make a fool of yourself.

And anyway, this is a waste of time.

End result: You believe it, so you don't draw.

That's why you might be feeling stressed at the very *idea* of drawing without somebody else's lines to color in. Believe me, you don't need any special talent or training in the arts to use this book. Any more than you do with a traditional stay-inside-the-lines coloring book.

1

I will provide drawing and writing prompts to help you express *from the inside out*. For forty years, art and writing prompts like the ones in this book have proven effective with my art therapy clients and students of all ages, from kindergarten through seniors. Research in the Garvey School District in Southern California (1981–82), and again in south Texas in the Edinburg Consolidated Independent School District (2014), has shown that activities like these reduce stress, improve health, enhance learning, and unblock creativity. In these studies students saw big academic gains and showed improvement in classroom behavior. In our 2014 Texas research, there were also health gains. No students came to the nurse's office on standardized testing day with headaches, vomiting, or diarrhea caused by test anxiety. Test stress is an epidemic problem in school districts in the United States. In these pilot research schools we applied the methods you are about to use in this book.

Relax! This is not an art class.

I'm not asking you to produce Art with a capital A. You won't be drawing for grades or someone else's approval. You won't be copying anyone else's art. And you can forget about exhibiting your drawings or meeting outside standards. This is *your* coloring book. What is drawn here stays here. And I will help you get past your Inner Critic who blocks your free expression of feelings, of creativity, and of your true self.

With *the new coloring book* you can:

Slow down.

Take time for yourself.

Scribble like you were in kindergarten.

Have fun doodling and drawing.

Express your true feelings and experiences in images.

Discover symbols that have personal meaning for you.

Find words for your moods and feelings.

Discover creative ways to effectively cope with stress.

Feelings in the Body

Emotions and worries often get stuffed into the body. Think about the common phrases we all use to describe this fact. And notice how *graphic* they are.

- She gives me a *head*ache.
- He's a pain in the *neck*.
- I had a lump in my *throat*.
- I'm carrying the weight of the world on my *shoulders*.
- I had butterflies in my *stomach*.
- My *knees* turned to jelly.

We also use *color* to describe physical and emotional reactions. We *feel* color in our bodies. We refer to colors as *warm*, such as, red, orange, and yellow. By contrast, we describe green, blue, and purple as cool colors. We talk about emotions through color: *green* with envy, *red* with rage, *yellow* (cowardly), feeling *blue*.

No Rules for Colors

You will be using colors to portray emotions in this book. There's no right or wrong color for expressing a feeling. There are no rules for what any color symbolizes or represents here. How you express through color is highly personal. Only *you* know what color is best to depict a mood or emotion of yours. If you ever learned any system of color symbolism, you can set it aside for these purposes. Color is very personal. When it comes to expressing feelings, colors mean different things to different people. The colors you choose are the *right* colors for *you*.

Releasing Stored Emotions

Emotions and worries that get stuck inside us cause trouble. If we don't *feel them* we can't *heal them*. They hide out in our body parts. The body becomes a closet full of unexpressed tensions, worries, fears, frustrations, anxiety, anger, sadness, and more. Emotions stored in the body cause stress. They pester us through pain, discomfort, irritability, or fatigue until we listen to them. If we don't listen, they keep calling out. Feelings just want to be listened to and accepted.

Feelings can be released from the body using the language of art. The important thing is to accept our feelings as being normal and natural. There are no "bad" emotions. We need to stop judging our feelings. We acknowledge them by literally *drawing them out of our bodies*. We do the same when we draw worrisome thoughts out of our minds. I will help you do this using art therapy principles to guide you.

What Is Art Therapy?

Art therapy is a form of psychotherapy and healing in which the client does expressive art-making. As with all professional therapy and counseling, art therapy is conducted by trained and credentialed individuals working with clients of all ages. The art made in art therapy is not Fine Art for display or for sale. It is very personal and kept private between the art therapist and the client. In art therapy sessions, individuals, families, or groups are gently guided through age-appropriate activities using a range of art materials. Art therapy is applied with children, adolescents, and adults of all ages and stages of life.

Art therapists guide their clients in expressing feelings, experiences, and insights through spontaneous art. Clients may explore their past, current challenges, nocturnal dreams, and life wishes. Instead of bottling emotions up and getting stressed or sick ("acting in") or allowing emotions to go out of control in destructive behavior ("acting out"), the client learns to express feelings safely, honestly, and creatively. The two- and three-dimensional art that results in a session is never critiqued from an esthetic point of view. It is used as a road map to the inner world of feelings, dreams, and wishes. The art therapist guides the client to reflect on his or her own insights and life lessons.

It's the *Process*, Not the Finished Product

By contrast to the process-oriented creations made in art therapy, Art (with a capital A) focuses on the *product*. I know because I have a degree in art and made a living as a professional artist and designer for years before becoming an art therapist. As artists, we were taught to work toward a finished product we could exhibit or sell. That is definitely not the case with the art produced in art therapy.

Much research has been published showing the effectiveness of art therapy (see the *Journal of the American Art Therapy Association*). Art therapy is used in treating a broad range of issues, such as natural and man-made disasters, trauma, marital and family conflicts, grief, and physical illness (cancer, Alzheimer's, and more). Clients find insights and learn coping skills they can use in any number of life situations. Art therapy is especially valuable for people who cannot speak or verbalize their feelings (young children, stroke patients, trauma survivors, and more). Art therapy is just as effective with people who have good language skills, but for another reason. These people often think and talk their way out of feelings. I have observed that it is easier for them to access emotions through right-brain methods, like art or movement therapy.

Becoming an art therapist requires a postgraduate degree in the field, followed by clinical supervision and experience along with certification by a qualified professional organization. In the United States it is the American Art Therapy Association. We also have the International Expressive Arts Therapy Association. I am an ATR and REAT registered with both these organizations.

Coloring Books Are NOT Art Therapy

To ethically call something art therapy requires a credentialed art therapist working with and guiding the client. Many popular adult coloring books claim to be art therapy. Using a coloring book may be therapeutic, just like cooking or a walk in the park can make one feel better. But it is not art therapy. Neither is this book art therapy (even though it uses art therapy principles). Remember, the purpose of art therapy is for clients to explore the inner life of feelings, dreams, and wishes and express it outwardly through art-making. Art therapists do not provide ready-made pictures or designs, as it would contradict the whole purpose of art therapy. There may be exceptions to this for a specific purpose, but they are exceptions.

Traditional coloring books may provide benefits. If coloring books help users feel calm and focused, that is a good thing. If coloring books help get people off electronic devices (to which many are addicted), that's a big step. And using your hands to draw on paper is a move in the right direction. The Draw-It-Yourself Coloring Book invites you to take the next step.

Coloring outside the Lines

In this book we go beyond the lines. In fact, we get rid of the lines altogether. Let's drop the "training wheels" on your emotions and creativity, so you can be free and fly. As I often say,

"If you want to think outside the box, stop coloring inside the lines."

This is as true of life as it is of coloring books. If you want a handmade, original, authentic life, you came to the right place. If you want to get past your Inner Critic who wants you to color inside other people's lines (in life and in coloring books), *this* is the book for you.

Artists have no advantage here.

Contrary to popular belief, when it comes to drawing feelings from the inside out for stress reduction and emotional release, trained or gifted artists may actually have a disadvantage. We artists are used to making art that looks good and gets appreciation or sales. Focusing only on the *process* for the purpose of personal growth is a foreign idea to most professional artists. Those of us with training and experience in art often approach art therapy and this type of spontaneous drawing with some uneasiness. Why? We are used to performing and focusing on the product.

Drawing from the inside out turns all the old art rules upside down and inside out.
(Pun intended.)

So relax, you nonartists. In many ways, you really have the advantage. You weren't trained in technique, so you are less likely to try to "perform." And anyway, we all have an Inner Art Critic to deal with, to one degree or another.

New Rules for the New Coloring Book

No external standards, no right or wrong.

Nothing to prove or accomplish.
(Wow!!! That makes me more relaxed just thinking about it.)

No one to please.
(These drawings are for your eyes only.)

There's no right or wrong way to draw in this book.
(You can't possibly make a mistake.)

No one will critique your work.
(The only goal here is to draw your stress out onto the paper.)

The only critic you have to deal with is the one in your own head.
(And I'll show you how to overcome that.)

Sometimes Art Happens

Once you've had the chance to draw in a safe, nonjudgmental atmosphere, you may find you enjoy drawing. Unlike coloring-in designs provided by others, here you will be coloring-in your own lines and pictures drawn from the *inside out*. This approach is about personal expression, self-observation, and (hopefully) insight. Here you can follow your own impulses and intuitions, and develop your own way of expressing what's inside. More important, you will be playing with art materials the way a child does.

If the Inner Artist Comes Out

Oftentimes, my art therapy clients or students uncover artistic talent they didn't know they had. It comes gushing out unexpectedly. It was either buried completely or had been consciously put in the closet because of outer criticism. Someone said, "You have no talent" or "Your art is ugly." Children and teens are often told that "art is frivolous and a waste of time." Boys frequently hear "art is for sissies." Many men tell me they heard this when they were boys and stopped drawing altogether. How sad! No wonder so many people are afraid to make art. But how liberated these people feel when they rediscover the Artist Within.

Whatever you do, just keep it fun and don't worry about the end results. The drawings in this book are coming from your Inner Child and are for you alone. They are not intended to "look pretty" or have aesthetic value according to preconceived standards of art. You wouldn't expect a kindergartner to produce Fine Art, so don't expect that of your Inner Child, either. Just enjoy yourself!

If you discover you are really enjoying art-making, you might be moved to do larger drawings or artwork. Consider branching out to sketchbooks or canvas, and exploring pastels, watercolors, acrylics, tempera, oil paint, collage, or even three-dimensional media like papier-mâché and clay. If the Art Spirit moves you, by all means follow it. Take some art classes, if you like, or attend a workshop. Or just do some art on your own. Whether or not you pursue art expression in other forms, when using *this book* please do not pressure yourself to perform or produce a "pleasing" product. This defeats the purpose of drawing your stress away.

How I Healed Myself through Drawing

Drawing helped save my life. Drawing my feelings out helped me heal from a life-threatening illness that had no cure. I have lived *the healing power of art* through firsthand experience. I also discovered that writing after drawing was immensely valuable. I gained insights and solved problems that had plagued me for a long time.

In recent years there has been research into the therapeutic value of writing out difficult emotions. A pioneering researcher, psychologist James W. Pennebaker, found that writing down one's feelings about an illness or traumatic event actually contributed to improved efficiency of the immune system. In a control-group study at Southern Methodist University in Dallas, Texas, blood samples were taken before a writing experiment, in which one group wrote about traumatic experiences, and again six weeks later. The experimental group who wrote about traumatic or difficult experiences *showed an enhanced ability to fight infection.* By contrast, blood samples from the control group, who wrote about trivial topics, showed no such strengthening of the immune system. Furthermore, *those who wrote about traumatic experiences made far fewer visits to the doctor* in the six-month period following the experiment. This research has been replicated in other studies with similar results.

The Healing Power of Your Other Hand

Many activities in this workbook include drawing and writing with the *nondominant* hand. The nondominant hand is the one you don't normally write with. I discovered this technique spontaneously while writing in my journal when I was seriously ill. It helped me heal without medication or medical intervention. Working with thousands of individuals, I have observed that writing with the nondominant hand taps directly into functions normally associated with the right hemisphere of the brain: emotional expression, sensory awareness, intuition, and creativity. As we know from decades of brain research, the right hemisphere of the brain specializes in nonverbal, visual-spatial functions, and emotional expression. Drawing and other visual arts rely greatly upon right brain processes. The same is true for mental imagery. Research has shown that the ability to express emotions relies heavily on right brain functions.

The left hemisphere of the brain processes verbal, mathematical, and logical information. It houses areas that govern the ability to follow rules of grammar, spelling, and syntax, and makes it possible for people to use a common language for communicating. If certain centers in the left hemisphere are damaged or diseased, speech and reading impairment will result. Our school systems and society as a whole emphasize verbal and logical processes (the three Rs: reading, writing, arithmetic; as well as science and technology). The arts, which develop right brain skills, are the most neglected and under-funded aspects of the curriculum in most school systems. The lack of art expression for children and teens can lead to "emotional illiteracy" (the inability to feel and express emotions effectively). No wonder there is so much violence and bullying in our schools today. We don't teach "emotional literacy."

What about Left-Handed People?

The right brain controls the entire left side of the body, while the left brain controls the right side of the body. Most people write with their right hand, the hand that is governed by the left (logical, verbal) side of the brain. However, some people who write with their right hand are actually "switch-overs." They were originally left-handed or ambidextrous and were forced by parents or teachers to be like everybody else and write with the right, "correct" hand.

Although it may not seem "logical," my clinical observations show that left-handed people as well as "switch-overs" get the same results as right-handed individuals when they write with their nondominant (nonwriting) hand. They too access creativity, intuition, and emotional expression (functions in which the right brain specializes). Science doesn't have an explanation for this yet, but I have volumes of data supporting this fact based on over forty years of experience observing thousands of individuals of all ages. For more about brain hemisphere functions, please see the TED talk online featuring Dr. Jill Bolte Taylor, author of *My Stroke of Insight*. After suffering a stroke in her left hemisphere, Taylor was immersed in right brain processing and describes it with great clarity. She had to regain left brain functions and so is able to talk and write about her experience of the right brain.

Brain Functions of the Two Hemispheres

Right	*Left*
Holistic	Order
Sees the big picture	Organization
In the moment	Time-based
Timeless	Reading
Feeling	Writing
Expressive	Syntax
Musical	Grammar
Artistic	Speech
Visual perception	Math
Creative	Reasoning
Emotionally expressive	Goal orientation
Sensory awareness	Analysis
Esthetic arrangement	Sequential logic
Body connection	Numbering
Physical sensing	Categorizing
Spatial perception	Linear thought
Dreaming	Makes "to do" lists
Sense of rhythm	Schedules
Intuitive	
Creative problem-solving	
Spiritual experience	

R L
Corpus Callosum

The corpus callosum is a bundle of nerve fibers connecting the two hemispheres of the brain. This enables the two sides to communicate. Writing with the nondominant hand has been shown to strengthen this connection. Activities in this book help you "let your left brain know what your right brain feels and needs."

Guidelines

1. Do activities **in the order given** when you use this book for the first time. If you repeat activities, choose the one that best meets your needs at the time. You can repeat these activities on loose paper or in a sketchbook.

2. Keep your Draw-It-Yourself Coloring Book **private and confidential**. You do not need to risk negative comments or criticism from others. Keep it in **a safe, private place** to ensure confidentiality. We're learning to tame the Inner Critic, so we don't need or want any criticism from outside.

3. **If you wish to share, be selective.** Share your Draw-It-Yourself Coloring Book only with people you trust, who are not critical of you or what you are doing, such as loved ones, therapists, or counselors. Be selective about what you share. Explain to them that this information is private and confidential and not to be passed on to others.

4. Honesty is the key. If you can't be honest with yourself, then you won't benefit from these techniques. That's why it's important to keep it confidential. If you're worried about what others will think, you'll edit yourself and not be honest.

5. A **quiet, private place** is best when using your Draw-It-Yourself Coloring Book.

Note: If you are a survivor of childhood abuse, have been diagnosed with posttraumatic stress disorder, or have a history of psychiatric disorders or treatment, it is advised that you use this Draw-It-Yourself Coloring Book with the guidance of a licensed mental health professional.

Materials

1. *Drawing Your Stress Away: A Draw-It-Yourself Coloring Book*

2. Art Materials

   • Colored markers (wide tip for drawing) in twelve or more assorted colors
   • A set of fine-point pens in assorted colors
   • Crayons in assorted colors

   Note: I do not recommend colored pencils, as I find they are not as effective for releasing emotions as crayons, markers, and pens. People tend to get too detailed and pictorial with colored pencils and forget about the purpose of drawing their stress out on paper. When strong emotions are being released, pencil lead easily breaks.

3. Unlined blank book or blank white paper, 8½ x 11 inches

If you find there is not enough blank paper in this Draw-It-Yourself Coloring Book, consider getting one of the following:

- Blank book (hardbound or paperback with unlined pages)
- Spiral-bound sketchpad with unlined paper
- Three-ring loose-leaf binder with unlined paper

Preparing to Use Your Draw-It-Yourself Coloring Book

Be sure that the place you've chosen is private, comfortable, and free from distractions.

No matter which activities you are on, it's a good idea to begin with a few slow deep breaths or one of your own favorite relaxation techniques. Relaxation breathing is restful and healing. It regenerates the body and mind and opens up awareness, intuition, and creativity.

Creative Draw-It-Yourself Coloring Book time

is your time to be alone with yourself.

Don't let anyone or anything encroach upon this very special time with yourself. For some, taking "alone time" may be difficult to do at first. Look at it this way: NOT taking time out *just for yourself* may be one of the reasons you feel stressed. So the first step toward de-stressing and feeling better is giving yourself this time. You deserve it!

Now you are ready to begin. Enjoy expressing your true self.

Part One

Thinking and Feeling on Paper

Visual art is a language of colors, shapes, textures, and lines. It is a language of its own. It is especially powerful for communicating feelings and intuitions that go beyond words. There are some feelings and inner experiences that simply cannot be expressed in verbal language. Literacy is usually defined as the ability to read and write. There is an equivalent in the language of art: *visual literacy*. Visual literacy is the ability to "read" art, feel it, understand it, and be moved by it, or not. Visual literacy also includes the ability to make art for esthetic decoration, communication, or therapy. Millions of people in our society consider themselves literate. It is generally accepted that almost anyone can be taught to read and write (with the exception of some individuals with handicaps). That belief is the cornerstone of public compulsory education. Literacy is not a question of "talent" or "creativity," but a matter of training. On the other hand, most people think they do not have the ability to draw. They believe that drawing is for people who have "talent," a mysterious ingredient (presumably in the genes) that one is either born with or lacks altogether. This simply is not true.

We all have the ability to draw until we are taught otherwise. This ability is a universal human characteristic. It is this same ability that enables us to write. So, if you can write, you can draw. If you can read, you can become visually literate. The fact is that visual art is far older than written words: drawing came before writing. Think about ancient cave paintings.

For many years I was a Head Start supervisor, a Montessori early education trainer, and instructor of child development on the college level. I observed thousands of children throughout the country from various ethnic and socioeconomic backgrounds. All the preschool-age children I observed drew naturally with spontaneity and exuberance. Once they started first grade, as time went on, most children began losing this natural urge and ability to express through art. Judgment or neglect of art kills it.

Sadly, we have forgotten visual literacy in our culture. Most people believe they cannot make art, so they do not. I have witnessed this over the years with my Creative Journal workshop participants and clients. Again and again, I have heard the vast majority say they "can't draw" and "don't have any talent." They are eager to write in their journals, but drawing is another matter altogether. Most of them get very nervous and fidgety when I tell them we are going to draw. They start giggling like teenagers and apologize *before they ever begin to draw.*

Earlier I described the roots of the "I can't draw" belief. A teacher, parent, sibling, or some authority figure had ridiculed or judged the individual's early attempts at drawing. A verdict had been delivered. That was the end of art for most. After all, who wants to be criticized and made fun of? Did that ever happen to you? If so, you are not alone. However, there is something you can do about it.

It is never too late to become visually literate, to learn the language of art. This does not mean becoming a professional or amateur "artist." You will learn how simple, spontaneous drawing can be a healing experience. It does not matter whether or not you think you have talent. There is nothing to compete for, no right or wrong way, and no good or bad drawings. You cannot possibly make a mistake! There are no standards to live up to and no judgments from outside.

The activities in this chapter introduce you to art as a therapeutic tool. You will be expressing emotions with color on paper—something every child knows how to do but most adults have forgotten. This is a safe and playful way to let off steam, release stress, and get in touch with your true feelings.

We begin with the most basic mode of drawing: scribbling, doodling, and making marks on paper just like you did as a little kid. We are not attempting to make symbols here. There is no intention to make a "pleasing" picture or a recognizable depiction of the three-dimensional world.

PLAYING ON PAPER

Relax and enjoy making marks on paper without expectations. Enjoy the process of exploring with colors; open up your right brain through drawing; use your whole brain by using both hands.

Materials: Colored markers, pens, crayons.

Use your **dominant hand** (the one you normally write with). Choose colors that feel good to you. Follow your instincts. Make marks, doodles, scribbles, or shapes on the following blank pages. Keep it simple. Do not try to make a representation or symbol of anything. Think of this as "warming up."

Use your **nondominant hand** (the one you do *not* normally write with). Continue playing with color below and on the following blank pages, to make your scribbles and doodles. If your Inner Art Critic starts chattering in your brain, ask it to go out for a break.

CALMING DOWN

Learn to meditate through drawing; relax and clear your mind;
enjoy the moment with no expectations or pressure to perform.

Materials: Colored pens, markers, crayons.

Drawing is a wonderful form of mindful meditation. Focusing and shutting out external distractions through art can be very calming and centering. For meditative drawing, you stay in the moment and experience the page in front of you as a world of its own. Take your time and go slowly.

Nondominant hand. Choose whatever color attracts you. Allow your pen or crayon to move across the page, drawing wherever your hand wants to go. Do not premeditate or plan what the drawing will look like. Stay out of your head. Let go of thoughts and concentrate on the page in front of you. Let your *hand* feel its way around the page, drawing spontaneously. If your mind wanders to thoughts of other things, just stop, go back to the present moment, and focus on the paper. Stay with your experience of the colors, lines, shapes, and textures your hand is making on the paper. Draw on the blank pages that follow.

Dominant hand. Now that you've made some drawings with your nondominant hand, write about the experience on this and the next page. How did it feel? Awkward, slow, silly, playful, fun? Did any thoughts cross your mind? What were they? Any judgments? Any memories?

Drawing is a form of emotional expression that can reach places words cannot go. There are some feelings and moods that simply will not translate into neat little phrases or sentences. At those times we are "speechless." We feel something, but have no words for it. Our mood defies verbal description. Because we have been trained to label things (in an attempt to understand and control them), this speechless state can feel uncomfortable. We may actually ignore the feelings because we do not have words for them. But the feelings do not go away. They have energy. They may fester in the dark. They hide out in our bodies only to appear later as symptoms of stress, physical or emotional illness. If that happens to you *a lot*, I recommend my book *Hello, This Is Your Body Talking*. Just like music and dance, drawing can be a wonderful way to release feelings. Here's your chance to express emotions in colors, lines, shapes, and textures on paper. This is the language of feelings.

DRAWING WITH FEELING

Release stored emotions; express feelings in the language of art;
tap into your right brain through your nondominant hand.

Materials: Colored pens, markers, crayons.

Sit quietly for a moment. Tune in to your feelings and allow yourself to experience them fully. If your feelings had colors, what would they be? Are they hot or cold colors? Do your feelings seem to have a shape? Do your feelings have a texture or a pattern? Do they have a rhythm as you make marks on the paper?

Nondominant hand. Find the answers to these questions by drawing your feelings out on paper. There are no right or wrong colors, only the ones that feel right for you. Draw spontaneously without judgment or concern for the finished product. Explore and experiment. Your picture does not have to look like anything in the outer world. It's okay to scribble, doodle, and make abstract shapes, lines, and patterns. This is an outward expression of your inner world of feelings.

The next time you are dealing with difficult feelings, such as fear, sadness, anger, depression, frustration, anxiety, or confusion, scribble them out on paper as you did in this exercise, using your *nondominant hand.*

Dominant hand. After you have completed your drawings, write your feelings out.

FEELINGS

*Express emotions through drawing; accept feelings without judging them;
translate emotions into art; learn "emotional literacy."*

Materials: Colored pens, markers, paper.

Nondominant hand. On the following blank pages do nine drawings, one each of nine commonly felt emotions listed below. Do not try to make pictures of anything recognizable. Play with color, line, shape, and texture to express these emotions. This is what young children do when they first start drawing: they scribble their feelings out.

Both hands. After drawing the emotion with your nondominant hand, complete the drawing by using both hands at the same time. Use two different colors.

Happy

Sad

Angry

Afraid

Playful

Loving

Confused

Depressed

Peaceful

SAD

33

ANGRY

AFRAID

35

CONFUSED

DEPRESSED

Nondominant hand. After drawing the nine feelings, write about the one that was the least comfortable for you.

Nondominant hand. Write about the feeling that you most enjoyed drawing.

A lot of research supports my clinical observations that stress is often a major factor in physical illness and emotional pain. Rush-hour traffic, job deadlines, overdue bills, health challenges, family crises, and news of natural and man-made disasters are only a few of the stress factors. We all need simple ways to release tension that builds up when living in a fast-paced and often violent and scary world.

GRAFFITI DRAWING

Release stress through drawing; express strong emotions; relax the body and mind.

Materials: Colored pens, markers, crayons, several sheets of paper.

Nondominant hand. Think of a stressful situation in your life. How does your body react to this stressful situation? Draw the stress out of your body by scribbling and making marks on paper. Choose colors that express how you feel about the situation. Don't try to make a picture of anything or represent people or objects in the outer world. Just scribble and doodle the feelings of stress freely out onto the page. Use as many sheets of paper as you need.

Note: If there are not enough blank pages provided here, use your own paper. If you have a blank journal, or sketchbook, do your extra scribbles there. You can also use computer paper, old newspapers, magazines, or scratch paper.

Nondominant hand. Write about the stressful situation you drew. How do you feel about it *after* doing the scribble drawings?

Part Two

Self-Care through Self-Expression

Healing the body and emotions starts with making friends with ourselves. It means learning to take tender loving care of our physical and emotional needs, our mental health, and our soul-life. If we have not been tuning in to our needs and being sure they get met, this can be challenging. Cancer survivors in our Creative Journal support groups who went into remission have said that simply taking quality time for themselves was a huge step toward well-being and peace of mind.

Listening to the "still small voice within" takes time. It takes quiet and a commitment to putting yourself first without labeling it "selfish," "egotistical," or thoughtless of others. When you take good care of yourself, you will have a lot more to give to others. Giving from a full cup *feels* better for everyone: the one giving and the one receiving.

The activities in this section help you give yourself permission to slow down, to "stop and smell the roses," and to be good to yourself.

De-stressing with Art

Oftentimes we feel like victims of circumstance, powerless to change certain areas of our lives. We think we will never get our bodies into shape, have fulfilling relationships, find a satisfying job, or get our finances in order. Not only do we fill our conversation with these negative statements, but we also fill our minds with negative mental pictures. These negative visualizations are self-fulfilling prophecies. The more we rerun those old "soap operas" in our minds, the more we talk about them, the more we make them a reality in our lives. The next exercise will help you repicture your life *the way you want it*.

*Identify stressful situations; change the picture from a negative one to a positive one;
use imagination to take charge of your life; create "visual affirmations."*

Materials: Crayons, colored pens, markers, paper.

Nondominant hand. On the next page, draw a picture of a stressful situation. Don't worry about making Art. Stick figures are fine. What does this stressful situation look like? What does it feel like? Do you feel trapped in a "box of duties"? Overwhelmed by a "mountain of work"? Attacked by "daggers of criticism"? Create a drawing that shows you and your experience of the situation.

New Life Pushes Up
(see written piece on page 52)

Nondominant hand. Look at your "stressful situation" drawing. Now draw a picture here of *how you would like the situation to feel*. Change the negative picture into a positive one. For instance, if you drew yourself under a mountain of work, you might now show yourself sitting contentedly on top of the mountain of completed work. Perhaps you add people who helped you complete the work.

Nondominant hand. Write in the present tense what it feels like to have resolved the stressful situation as pictured in drawing #2. Example: *I feel great. I'm grateful to have gotten the help I needed. Having mentors made it so much less stressful. I feel more relaxed and energetic.*

(Written piece accompanying drawing on page 48)

New Life Pushes Up

Political upheaval, economic uncertainty, bigotry, angry rhetoric. And it's hotter than hell outside.

It all weighs heavily on me as I drive to my weekly "Mindfulness in Art" class.

"Today we'll go a little deeper," the teacher says, "letting whatever wants to rise up spill out onto the paper. Not from up here," she continues, tapping her forehead with her index finger. "Don't think. Feel."

The brush moves in my hand, collecting color and laying it down. Jagged black lines rend the empty white field of paper.

My stomach hurts. My head resists. *I don't want to be here this morning. I should be home writing. I wish I hadn't signed up for this class. This is a waste of time.*

The brush keeps moving. Bruises rise in black and blue, like mountains too tired to stand any longer. Parched, cracked earth mutates into broken bones. The ravaged multitudes cry enough! no more! as flames of collapse and destruction blaze hotter and higher.

None of this comes from "up here" in my head. The brush moves first, the story comes after.

Fifty dead in an attack on a gay nightclub. Two more black men die at the hands of police. Terrorists attack an airport in Istanbul. California burns while West Virginia floods. Deadly tornado in China and a super typhoon bearing down on Taiwan. The presidential election resembles a circus act as we once more contemplate our civil duty to vote for the lesser of two evils.

Somewhere above this battered broken plain of pain and dysfunction a light shines. It beckons. New green life pushes up through the torn earth, growing from the wounded place, watered with our tears.

Drawing to Music

Like dancing, drawing to music tends to keep you in the *present* moment instead of the future, in the *process* instead of the outcome. It definitely quiets your left (logical/verbal) brain and sparks your right brain. This is a very kinesthetic approach to drawing, in which you use your whole body, not just your arms, hands, and eyes. After drawing to music, many workshop participants discuss how the music affected them while they were drawing. They say things like:

"I stopped worrying about how the drawing looked and concentrated on the feelings in my body."

"The music just relaxed me so I was not so uptight and critical of what I was drawing."

"The music took my mind off my expectations of how the drawing should turn out. I got into the colors and the sounds and forgot about my mental thoughts."

DANCING ON PAPER

Relax with music and movement; combine auditory and kinesthetic expression with visual-art experience; use drawing as movement to music; "dance on paper."

Materials: Large sheets of newsprint paper (18"× 24"); colored pens, markers, crayons. Optional: oil pastels or chalk pastels in assorted colors. Your choice of music: preferably expressing a variety of moods and tempos.

In a place where you can be completely alone, do some spontaneous movement to music. Select music that fits your mood. Allow your *body* to respond to the music, not your critical mind that wants you to look good or acceptable to others. Listen to the music with your whole body, improvising and playing with the rhythm and the melody. If you find yourself reverting back to structured or traditional dance steps, just be aware of it and go back to improvising and finding your own dance. Do this for a few minutes or as long as you like.

Nondominant hand. As you continue playing the music, start drawing to it. Let the music flow through you. Use colors you associate with the sounds and rhythms. Express any feelings that the music brings up. Choose the appropriate drawing tool for each musical passage. It may be easier to interpret one piece of music with crayons and another with colored pens. Also, try using both hands at the same time. If you need more pages than are provided here, use your own paper.

Dominant hand. Write about the Dancing on Paper experience.

Identify a current challenge or problem; picture a solution to the challenge or problem.

Materials: Colored pens, markers, crayons.

Nondominant hand. Draw a picture of a "problem" situation in your life. It can be an abstract picture, a cartoon, or a simple depiction.

Dominant/nondominant hands. Let the "problem" speak to you. Does it have a name? Have a "conversation" with the "problem" that's bothering you. Write the following questions with your ***dominant hand.*** Let the "problem" respond by writing with your ***nondominant hand***.

Here are the questions to ask.

- What or who are you?
- How do you feel?
- What has caused you to feel this way?
- How can I help you? What do you want me to do for you?
- What can I learn from this?

Nondominant hand. Draw the solution to this problem. Show how you would like things to be.

A SAFE PLACE—1

Use creative imagination to picture safety and comfort; create images that bring relaxation and peace.

Materials: Colored pens, markers, crayons.

Nondominant hand. On the next page, draw a picture of a place that feels safe, protected, and comfortable. It can be a place you've been or one you imagine. It might be inside (a cozy room), a place in nature, a church or temple. Think of it as a place where nothing bad can happen to you. Make a photocopy of your "safe place" drawing and put it up where you can see it each day.

Nondominant hand. Write about how it feels to be in your personal safe place as depicted in your drawing.

YOUR PERSONAL POWER SYMBOL

Create a meaningful symbol for your own inner strength; visualize protection in difficult situations.

Materials: Colored pens, markers, crayons.

Nondominant hand. On the next page, draw an image of your own personal power. Think of it as your power symbol. This image can come in the form of an animal, an object, something from nature, a person, or a spiritual symbol (a cross, a Star of David, an Om symbol, etc.). Choose a symbol that gives you the feeling of protection and strength. In difficult situations, picture this symbol in your mind and feel the strength that it represents for you. You can photocopy this picture and display it so you can see it daily.

Increase your awareness of the difference between relaxation and tension; become aware of tension in particular parts of your body; experience your tension level and learn to relax quickly and effectively.

Materials: Colored pens, markers, crayons.

Nondominant hand. On this page, draw a picture of *tension*. This can be an abstract design or doodle. It can be a symbolic portrait or cartoon of yourself feeling tense or in a tense situation. If you experience different kinds of tension in different situations, create more than one drawing of *tension* using the next page.

Nondominant hand. Let your "tension" drawing speak. Write down what it says. Let it tell you how it feels, what causes it, and what you can do about it.

Lie down or sit in a comfortable chair. Starting at your feet, tense them up as much as possible and then let go completely. Tense and relax your feet, legs, and torso. Then let go. Tense and relax your shoulders, neck, arms, and hands. Then let go. Repeat this with your head and face. Enjoy being relaxed.

Nondominant hand. After you have experienced relaxing fully, draw a picture of *relaxation* on the next page. This can be an abstract design, a doodle, or a picture of yourself being relaxed.

Dominant hand. Write about *relaxation* as shown in your picture. How does being relaxed feel in your body? How does it feel emotionally?

Dominant hand. What do you do to relax? What works best for you? Are there other ways to relax that you would like to explore? Write down some new ways to relax.

It is very difficult to remain "speedy" when writing or drawing in slow motion. This kind of meditative writing and drawing has a self-hypnotic effect and calms the mind and body. However, it is important that you write messages that are positive and relaxing.

SLOWING DOWN

Learn to cope with feeling hyperactive or nervous; allow your mind to relax its fear-thoughts.

Materials: Colored pens or markers.

Nondominant hand. Write your name on this page *as slowly as you possibly can*. For instance, take five minutes to write your first and last names. Then write a brief relaxing message to yourself, such as: "Slow down" or "Take it easy" or "Relax." Write in slow motion so the pen is barely moving. Repeat the above activity with your **dominant hand.**

Nondominant hand. Scribble or doodle in slow motion. Take a few minutes to make a line or shape. Let your hand wander aimlessly around the page as you draw. Consciously slow down as much as possible.

Dominant hand. Once again scribble or doodle in slow motion. Consciously slow down as much as possible.

REST AND RELAXATION—1

Reflect upon and inventory your current life; replenish your energy and restore yourself; develop the ability to daydream; achieve a centered and peaceful state of being.

Materials: Colored pens, markers, crayons.

Nondominant hand. With your eyes closed, do some deep breathing. Ask yourself: *What do I do for rest and relaxation?* On this page, draw pictures of things you do for R&R.

Dominant hand. Now think of some new ways of relaxing. Include pets or other important elements in your life. Add these to the appropriate lists below.

PEOPLE, PETS, OR THINGS	PLACES	ACTIVITIES

Nondominant hand. Draw pictures of yourself making your life more restful and relaxing. Be practical and specific. Implement your plans. Put them in your calendar or schedule. Check back in a few days to see how you're doing.

A BEAUTIFUL PLACE

Use visualization for relaxation and peace of mind.

Materials: Colored pens, markers, crayons.

When you're stressed, take time to do this. Recall a beautiful place you have visited, one in which you felt calm and peaceful. Picture the beautiful place in your mind's eye. Look all around you and take in the surroundings through your senses. See the objects, shapes, and colors. Feel the textures. Smell the fragrances. Hear the sounds around you. Sense the general atmosphere. Now close your eyes, picture the beautiful place, and allow yourself to relax fully and enjoy this environment.

Nondominant hand. On the next page, draw a picture of yourself feeling calm and peaceful in your beautiful place.

WHERE THE TIME GOES: A MANDALA

Examine your current priorities by re-evaluating use of time; plan for less stress with specific needs and goals in mind; take better charge of your time instead of feeling like a helpless victim of the clock.

Materials: Colored pens, markers, crayons.

Dominant hand. On the next page, make a list of all your life activities (see example below). Next to each activity, write down the approximate number of hours in a typical week you devote to that activity.

Activities

Sleeping	Commuting, traveling	Hobbies
Eating	Working	Entertainment
Food preparation, shopping, etc.	Socializing	Education
Personal grooming	Recreation	Spiritual practices
Household maintenance	Physical exercise	Other

Dominant hand. Create a mandala (Sanskrit word for circle) by drawing a large circle and dividing it into wedge-shaped pieces, each representing an item on your list from the previous page (see the example below). The size of each piece is determined by the percentage of time you devote to that activity.

Nondominant hand. Draw images or symbols in each wedge depicting that item on your list.

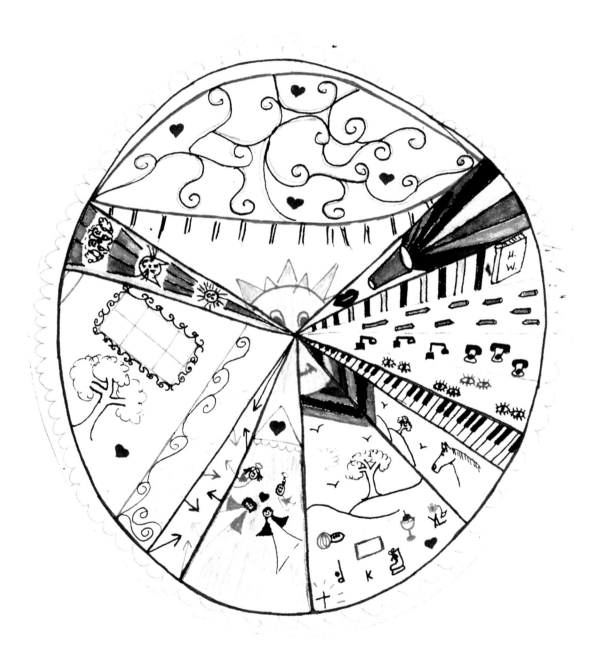

Dominant hand. Check your priorities at the present time. If you'd like to make changes, make a new list showing how you would *like* to spend your time.

Nondominant hand. Now draw a new circle and fill it in, reflecting your priorities.

Dominant hand. Make a one-week calendar and fill in the new activities based on your second mandala. Indicate the amount of time devoted to each. Then write about how you will implement the changes in your everyday life. Give special attention to health-oriented and self-care activities.

SPECIAL TREATS—1

Cultivate self-appreciation; identify things you like to do; be good to yourself; schedule treats into your calendar.

Materials: Colored pens, markers, crayons.

Dominant hand. Make a list of special treats you'd like to give yourself.

Nondominant hand. Draw pictures of the special treats you want to give yourself.

Dominant hand. Each day, give yourself *at least* one special treat. Plan your treats at the beginning of the day or week. Create a "treats" calendar (see below) on the following page for the next week and *do* the items entered there. Each week add more treats.

Example:

Saturday: Sleep in, breakfast in bed, take a bubble bath, a walk in the park, etc. . . .

Sunday: Lunch out with friends

Monday: Buy that book I've been wanting

Tuesday: Go out to a movie with friends

A DAY OFF—1

Set aside routine; treat yourself to activities you truly enjoy; say "I love you" to yourself; find out what makes you feel good; give yourself what you enjoy.

Materials: Colored pens, markers, crayons.

Plan a day off. Plan to do things you enjoy but don't normally do. Find activities that are relaxing, inspiring, energizing, etc. If possible, do not work or do chores on that day. Let this truly be a day off, a mini-vacation from routine and duty. List things you can do specifically to relieve any tension you are carrying. Try a massage, hot bath, meditation, yoga, walking in nature, etc.

Then take your day off and actually *do* the things you planned. If you think you can't take an entire "day off," start with a half-day.

Nondominant hand. Write or draw out your plans.

Nondominant hand. Write about your day off. What was it like? Did you do the things you planned? Were you resistant? Did you fill up the day with chores and other routine activities?

Nondominant hand. Plan another day off. Let this one be different. Make it a spontaneous day with no planning. Just let yourself relax and flow with your feelings on that particular day. Ask yourself: How do I feel and what do I feel like doing today? Be good to yourself!

Repeat the "day off" exercise on a regular basis—once a week, once a month, etc.

Identify the negative statements you make about your health or yourself;
transform negative thoughts into life-affirming statements.

Materials: Colored pens, markers, crayons.

Dominant hand. List negative statements you often make about yourself or your life. *"I never have enough money." "I will never lose this extra ten pounds." "My boss drives me crazy." "I do all the work and get no credit." "Nobody appreciates what I do for them."*

NEGATIVE STATEMENTS

Nondominant hand. Instead of describing what you *do not* want, you will now describe (and eventually create) what you *do want*. Rewrite each negative statement from the previous page so that it clearly states what you *do want*. Use the present tense, as if it were already a reality.

Example: *"I never have enough money"* becomes *"I always have whatever I need."*

HOW I WANT IT TO BE

Create a new attitude; rewrite your negative beliefs; take charge of your mind and thoughts.

Nondominant hand. Draw a picture for each of your new positive beliefs. Caption each picture with the positive statement or affirmation. You can create this in small boxes, like a comic strip.

Each day observe what you say about your life and your health. When you hear yourself saying something negative, stop and think about the belief that your words express. Ask yourself if you want to *reinforce* the belief, or if you want to *change* it. If you decide to *change* it, *speak* your new belief. Better yet, draw it as well.

Stressful situations will always be there. That's life. How we respond to stress is up to us. It's the only thing we can have control over. De-stressing is an ongoing process. You now have more tools for dealing with stress. You can always repeat these prompts as needed using a sketchbook or a loose-leaf binder. These techniques will travel with you. There is no expiration date.

If physical challenges come up, acute illness, surgery, chronic conditions, or treatment for diseases like cancer, consider using my Draw-It-Yourself Coloring Book entitled *Hello, This Is Your Body Talking*. In cancer support groups my associates and I have led, we have seen amazing emotional resilience develop in our members as they use the methods presented in both of these books. I've used these techniques to cope with two hip replacements and recovery from serious injury. Of course, these books are not substitutes for professional medical or mental health care, but the drawing and writing prompts can help you deal with the emotional side of illness.

Thank you for allowing me to accompany you on this journey of well-being. It is my hope that you will continue to create a life that supports your health: physical, emotional, mental, and spiritual. May you be guided to let go of stressors that are expendable and deal creatively with the new ones that come up. May you continue reshaping how you handle stress by drawing and writing from the inside out.

May these techniques help you put into action what you learn from that "still, small voice within": your own inner wisdom that speaks through your drawings and writings. Be well!

Recommended Reading & Listening

Abaci, Peter. *Conquer Your Chronic Pain: A Life-Changing Drug-Free Approach for Relief, Recovery, and Restoration.* Wayne, NJ: New Page Books, 2016.

Capacchione, Lucia. *Visioning: Ten Steps to Designing the Life of Your Dreams.* New York: Tarcher/Putnam, 2000.

———. *The Power of Your Other Hand: A Course in Channeling the Inner Wisdom of the Right Brain.* Wayne, NJ: Career Press, 2001.

———. *The Art of Emotional Healing.* Boston, MA: Shambhala, 2006.

———. *The Picture of Health* (Audio/CD). Cambria, CA: luciac.com, 2006.

———. *The Creative Journal: The Art of Finding Yourself (35th Anniversary Edition).* Athens, OH: Swallow Press/Ohio University Press, 2015.

———. *Hello, This Is Your Body Talking: A Draw-It-Yourself Coloring Book.* Athens, OH: Swallow Press/Ohio University Press, 2017.

Chapman, Linda. *Neurobiologically Informed Trauma Therapy with Children and Adolescents: Understanding Mechanisms of Change.* New York: Norton, 2014.

Cooper, Jessie Allen. *The Sound of Feelings Sampler* (Audio/CD). Everett, WA: Cooper Sound Waves, 2007 (available at luciac.com).

Gopalan, Radha. *Second Opinion: How to Combine Eastern and Western Medical Philosophies to Increase Your Wellness and Healing Power.* Scottsdale, AZ: Plata Publishing, 2015.

Nakazawa, Donna Jackson. *Childhood Disrupted: How Your Biography Becomes Your Biology, and How You Can Heal* (New York: Simon & Schuster, 2015).

Pennebaker, James W. *Opening Up: The Healing Power of Confiding in Others.* New York: Avon Books, 1990.

———. *Writing to Heal: A Guided Journal for Recovery from Trauma and Emotional Upheaval.* Oakland, CA: New Harbinger, 2004.

Pert, Candace B. *Molecules of Emotion: Why You Feel the Way You Feel*. New York: Scribner, 1997.

———. *Everything You Need to Know to Feel Go(o)d*. Carson, CA: Hay House, 2006.

Sarno, John E. *The Mindbody Prescription: Healing the Body, Healing the Pain*. New York: Warner Books, 1998.

Siegel, Daniel J. *Mindsight: The New Science of Transformation*. New York: Norton, 2010.

van der Kolk, Bessel A. *The Body Keeps the Score: Brain, Mind, and Body in the Healing of Trauma*. New York: Viking, 2014.